Naveen
Nannapaneni

737-0103

SLAM DUNK SUPERSTARS

SLAM DUNK SUPERSTARS

PETER C. BJARKMAN

Crescent Books
New York/Avenel, New Jersey

This 1994 edition published by Crescent Books, distributed by
Random House Value Publishing, Inc.,
40 Engelhard Avenue,
Avenel, New Jersey 07001

Random House
New York • Toronto • London • Sydney • Auckland

Produced by
Brompton Books Corporation
15 Sherwood Place
Greenwich, CT 06830

ISBN 0-517-12035-6

8 7 6 5 4 3 2 1

Printed and bound in China

For my son, Chris Bjarkman, a firefighter who knows his own brand of action.

PAGE 1: Shaquille O'Neal represents the new generation of powerful slam dunkers who thrill today's NBA fans.

PAGE 2: Michael Jordan has taken basketball's most thrilling move to new heights with his patented hangtime flights above the rim.

RIGHT: Chicago Bulls' star Scottie Pippen slams home a monster dunk with typical authority.

CONTENTS

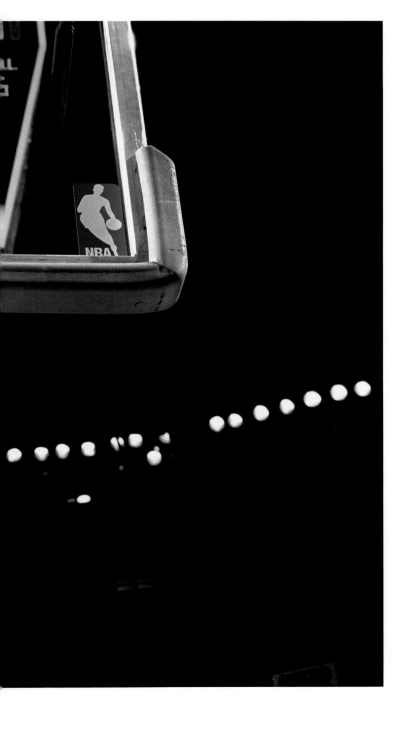

INTRODUCTION

If it is true that professional basketball has replaced backward-looking baseball and violence-laden football as the game of choice for a whole new generation of American youngsters and oldsters, then it is probably also true that the exciting slam dunk shot has much to do with this sudden trading of allegiances. It is the soaring grace, elevating freedom and electrifying finality of the dunk shot, after all, that seems most in tune with the pulse of today's sports-hungry fans.

Surely it is the undeniable individual artistry – as well as the more obvious instantaneous gratification of the dunk – which also explains its universal appeal in the modern era of televised sports. While the dunk now enjoys the same prominence on the basketball court that the home run long held on the baseball field, it is also the "masters of dunk" who now occupy a spotlight of stardom reserved in the national pastime for home run sluggers. With basketball, it is the highest flyers and most authoritative slam-jammers who are the biggest superstars. Television highlight films endlessly feature rim-crunching dunks, not the three-point bombs or needle-threading passes that were the big attraction of the game's earlier days. Dunkers are the athletes who today indisputably rule America's most rapid-fire game.

Although the dunk is the rage of today's NBA and

OPPOSITE: Isaiah Rider of the Timberwolves performs an "East Bay Funk Dunk" en route to capturing the 1994 Gatorade Slam Dunk title before the home crowd at the Minneapolis Target Center Arena.

RIGHT: Often thought of as a shot-swatting defender, Patrick Ewing can also provide instant offense with his rim-rattling and net-ripping slams.

college hoop game, it is not an offensive strategy entirely new to a sport which began with peach baskets and set shots a century ago. Dunking indeed has a long and colorful heritage in the history of professional basketball. Bill Russell of the invincible Boston Celtics led by Red Auerbach was the first to incorporate the occasional dunk into his offensive arsenal. The 7-foot Wilt Chamberlain dunked also, but his game often featured a softer touch around the hoop. Wilt was more likely to drop from the hoop and convert a soft fadeaway jumper which defenders six inches shorter had no hope of blocking. One can only wonder what the towering Chamberlain might be like today, when dunking and slamming and hanging on the rim are standard fare. For when Russell and "Wilt the Stilt" ruled the infant days of pro hoops, the age of "hangtime" was hardly yet in vogue.

The game's big men were not the ones, in the end, who pioneered today's awesome dunking style of

ABOVE: Even in basketball's primitive era of the 1950s Wilt Chamberlain (here with the University of Kansas) was providing a glimpse of things to come once the game went fully airborne.

OPPOSITE LEFT: Dr. J (Julius Erving), who wrote the book on hangtime moves, here demonstrates his unique style in the 1984 NBA Slam Dunk Contest.

play. That was left to a generation of small forwards and big guards who took over the courts in the wake of Russell's dynasty Celtics. One was Gus "Honeycomb" Johnson, now all but forgotten to basketball history. Johnson, a muscular 6'6" leaper with the NBA Baltimore Bullets of the early '60s, was the first to dislodge a backboard and rim in the heat of game action. And while Johnson enjoyed only a brief moment of celebrity for his rare destructive feat, another of the game's greatest acrobats also made his mark in the days before primetime tele-

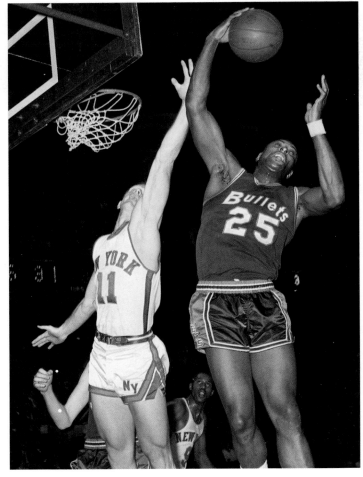

TOP RIGHT: Even before Julius Erving there was playground and NBA legend Connie Hawkins, seen here in 1975 slamming one home for the Atlanta Hawks late in his all-too-brief NBA career.

RIGHT: Leaping Gus "Honeycomb" Johnson of the Baltimore Bullets, seen here in 1966 action, was the first to break an NBA backboard. He did so with an awesome pre-season exhibition slam in his 1963 rookie year.

vised play. Connie Hawkins owned more solo moves than any playground star who ever dribbled and dunked. It was "The Hawk" – cradling the ABA's red, white and blue ball in his huge hands – who truly popularized a new style of solo flights to the hoop. And he did it years before Julius Erving and decades before Michael Jordan.

Then there was the athlete who revolutionized basketball forever by taking the game permanently above the rim – the one who came to be known simply as "Doctor" – Julius Erving. Erving remains the unchallenged master if not the stylistic inventor of slam dunking as a recognized basketball art form. The man celebrated as "Doctor" is the original high flyer – the lionized player who more than any other pioneered the free-flying and gravity-defying game of modern pro hoops. Before Erving came along, the hardwood sport was still largely earthbound and even waning in popularity.

When Dr. J first arrived in the American Basketball Association as a little-known star player from the University of Massachusetts, he brought with him a remarkable new kind of offense that would turn heads and open eyes everywhere. By the time he had become an established star with the Philadelphia Sixers of the NBA all other high flyers would forevermore be compared only to him.

OPPOSITE TOP LEFT: The soaring grace of Dr. J has now been replaced by the crunching power of Shaquille O'Neal – one of basketball's latest slam dunk superstars.

OPPOSITE TOP RIGHT: The signature work of the man-mountain they call "Shaq" was this crushed basket stanchion in New Jersey's Meadowlands Arena.

OPPOSITE BOTTOM RIGHT: David Robinson gives his own meaning to the 1990s' version of "hangtime." In 1994 Robinson of the San Antonio Spurs became the first center in over 20 long seasons to lead the NBA in scoring.

LEFT: Darryl Dawkins of the Philadelphia Sixers pioneered a new style of power slam in the late '70s and early '80s which he colorfully labelled the "Chocolate Thunder" slam.

Clyde Drexler, Patrick Ewing, Alonzo Mourning and others are the bold skywalkers who today advance Julius Erving's colorful one-on-one playground style to glamorous new heights all around the NBA circuit. "Sir Charles" Barkley, Shawn Kemp and "Shaq-Attaq" O'Neal have already carved their niche with a thunderous new rim-jarring style, while Scottie Pippen, Otis Thorpe, Dominique Wilkins and Harold Miner consistently defy gravity with their soaring ballet-like hangtime leaps.

Dozens of other young stars throughout the league have now joined the high-flying dunker's game. Nothing in today's world of professional basketball so electrifies a crowd and so inspires the players themselves as the soaring and crashing of a perfectly executed "hangtime" slam. This is the true "signature move" of America's native game and the world's fastest and most thrilling sport. These pages celebrate the feats of basketball's highest flyers, those few incredible athletes who elevate our imaginations as well as our pulses with each new solo flight, and even suggest with their gyrations above the hoop that perhaps man was not meant to be entirely earthbound after all.

Michael Jordan
Chicago Bulls

Nickname: **"Air" Jordan**
Height: **6'6"**; Position: **Guard**
College: **University of North Carolina**
Drafted: **Chicago, 1984**

"Michael does it better in real life than I ever did it in my dreams." **RICK BARRY,** NBA SUPERSTAR

Despite his premature retirement, Air Jordan indeed merits the widely applied label as the most astounding athlete in basketball annals, and perhaps in the annals of all sports history. Julius Erving two decades earlier had set a standard for a soaring and leaping playing style which every subsequent player – from playground to pro arena – aimed to copy and make his own. Michael Jordan, as well, fashioned a personal style of airborne acrobatics on the hardwood which kept fans and rivals alike in perpetual awe. Basketball has never before seen quite so complete an athlete and showman in its first half-century; it is likely that the sport will never see another like him in its second half-century either.

Michael Jordan's legacy will always reside par-

LEFT: Air Jordan sails by the hoop seconds before releasing a windmill slam in the finals of the 1988 Gatorade Slam Dunk match-up at Chicago Stadium. It was in this competition that Jordan won his second Slam Dunk championship crown.

OPPOSITE: It was moves like this one against Magic and the Los Angeles Lakers that always seemed to make Michael's scoring totals and other statistics secondary to the show that he put on nightly in NBA arenas for nine magical seasons.

OPPOSITE LEFT: Michael stuffs two of his 36 points during the second game of the 1988 Eastern Conference semifinal series with Detroit. This series would represent the last time the Bulls and Jordan would be eliminated from post-season action before the start of their glorious three-peat championship run.

OPPOSITE RIGHT: Some now contend Air Jordan was the greatest basketball player ever, while others still cast their ballots for Oscar Robertson or Wilt "The Stilt" Chamberlain. But none disputes that Jordan was basketball's first true international celebrity megastar.

LEFT: Jordan's thunderous slams were as much a part of NBA championship play as they were of slam dunk exhibitions and endless regular season contests. Here Michael punctuates a jam shot in the second quarter of Game 5 during the 1991 championship series versus Los Angeles.

tially in his unmatchable numbers. No other NBA player has ever boasted a higher career scoring average (32.3), only Wilt Chamberlain has won an equal number of league scoring titles (seven consecutive) and only Wilt (four times) has surpassed Jordan's single-season average of 37 ppg. No one else has been MVP of the championship finals for three straight years and no one else has scored as many points (63) in a single NBA playoff game. No pro player has ever scored more consecutive points (23) in any single game. And no offensive star has ever been as honored or celebrated as well at the defensive end of the court, where Jordan three times led the league in steals, was tabbed "Defensive Player of the Year" (1988), and was named to the all-NBA Defensive First Team in each of his final six campaigns.

Like Dr. J and Oscar Robertson of past NBA generations, Michael Jordan is remembered everywhere for his indelible image and unmatchable

style, and not merely for the numbers he relentlessly posted. He may have in the end fallen a hairbreadth short of Oscar Robertson as the game's greatest all-around player. He joined the distinguished ranks of Julius Erving, Wilt Chamberlain and George Mikan as a player whose impact on the game changed the sport forever. Yet unlike those forerunners he was blessed by playing in basketball's great television age, and thus he soared to the top as America's most glamorous and recognized sports hero since baseball's Babe Ruth. There has never been another hoopster who did more to popularize the game of basketball worldwide. Jordan will always remain entrenched among the half-dozen or so miraculous players known as basketball's greatest legends.

LEFT: Jordan raises his fist in triumph seconds after the Bulls nailed down a three-peat 1993 world championship in Phoenix.

BELOW: A highlight moment of Jordan's glorious career came with his first NBA title. Michael here hugs the trophy that had for so long eluded him.

OPPOSITE: Sacramento's Arco Arena is the scene for this version of "Air Jordan" hangtime. Bulls teammate Horace Grant trails the play for the rebound that will not be necessary.

Charles Barkley

Phoenix Suns

Nickname: **"Sir Charles"**
Height: **6'6"**; Position: **Forward**
College: **Auburn University**
Drafted: **Philadelphia, 1984**

"There will never be another player like me again. I'm the ninth wonder of the world." –
CHARLES BARKLEY

During the 1993 NBA playoff finals Charles Barkley made certain there was almost as much excitement off the court as there was during the games themselves. Barkley drew attention just as he always has, with his colorful and sometimes shocking public statements. "Sir Charles" was at his best with the media during the spotlight of championship play. "There will never be another player like me again," Barkley warned the press. "I'm the ninth wonder of the world."

While his outrageous bragging may often seem overdone, Barkley always seems to have the wherewithal to back up even the most exaggerated boasts. When he left Auburn University in 1984 he owned the fourth highest scoring mark in school history. His collegiate trophy case also holds a plaque for the Southeastern Conference "Player of the Decade" for the 1980s. Over a full decade of NBA play the man dubbed "the round mound of rebound" has picked up steam as an unstoppable

OPPOSITE: Fans, coaches, writers and opposing players all continue to marvel at the physical play of Charles Barkley. No other big man has ever been quicker, more agile, or more able to run the court and fly above the rim. It is moves like this end-to-end solo against Portland which suggest that Barkley is indeed "the ninth wonder of the world" – just as the colorful "Sir Charles" has claimed.

RIGHT: There is quickness as well as power to Barkley's game. Here the incomparable Phoenix franchise player looks for an opening around Seattle center Michael Cage. It is the all-around game of this fearsome power forward that earned him four straight selections to the All-NBA First Team (1988-1991) as well as an MVP Award at the 1991 NBA All-Star Game.

LEFT: Chicago's Stacey King is victimized by a typical Barkley power slam in Game 5 of the 1993 NBA Finals. It was moves like this that allowed Barkley to record more dunks (917) than any other player in the six-year span between 1987 and 1993. The "biggest small forward" in the game, Barkley is not only an offensive whirlwind but an unstoppable rebounding force as well, averaging more than 800 boards per season over his 10-year NBA career.

OPPOSITE: A rare moment in NBA history occurred during the 1992 Slam Dunk competition. A new dunking legend was born when Cedric Ceballos strapped on a blindfold in Orlando and soared toward the hoop for his winning "Hocus Pocus" slam-jam.

force from one end of the court to the other. Among his overflowing credentials are: better than 800 rebounds a season, four consecutive All-Star Game starts and six overall appearances, better than 23 ppg in both regular and post-season play, and above 16,000 career points and 8,000 career rebounds.

Barkley has always been controversial both off and on the court. In Philadelphia when playing for the Sixers he often publicly criticized his owner and his teammates for not wanting to win badly enough. Charles has always put winning and hustling at the very top of his personal goals. But the outspoken athlete has also had important and serious messages for his legions of fans. Recently he made a television commercial in which he tells young fans that he should not be a hero or an idol just because he can dribble and shoot. Youngsters should use their own parents and teachers as role models, not glamorous ballplayers, Barkley warns.

On the court, however, Sir Charles has always had a personal style which has made him a widely recognized star. He is one of basketball's most ferocious rebounders and has averaged more than 800 for each of his nine seasons. The most memorable aspect of Barkley's play is his unbounded fierceness under the basket and anywhere around the rim. The typical Barkley maneuver is to grab a defensive rebound, lumber the full length of the court like a runaway truck, then slam home a huge dunk that intimidates his foes and electrifies the crowd. Indeed the most terrifying sight in basketball – perhaps in all of sports – has to be the image of this huge and agile 250-pound athlete roaring down the floor toward the enemy basket, daring any defender to block his path. With his large but finely tuned body Barkley has been the most physical player of the past decade. His personal style has also made him one of the game's greatest and most notorious stars.

Cedric Ceballos

Phoenix Suns

Nickname: **"Ice"**
Height: **6'6"**; Position: **Forward**
College: **California State University, Fullerton**
Drafted: **Phoenix, 1990**

"If he really couldn't see, I really don't see how he could have done it." – MICHAEL JORDAN, after Cedric Ceballos's blind-folded jam at the 1992 NBA Slam Dunk Contest

Some legends are built over years of stellar performance, while some are earned in an eye-blink, perhaps during a single moment of brilliant athleticism or a single demonstration of unprecedented achievement. Cedric Ceballos is one of those who earned his place in slam dunk lore with a single solo encore of stunning brilliance.

No player has gained quite as much notoriety from a single outing in the Gatorade Slam Dunk showcase as has the Suns' second-round selection from the 1990 draft. Cedric Ceballos seized on his moment in the NBA exhibition spotlight and left an undying impression. The setting was the Orlando Coliseum in February 1992 and the final round of dunking had come down to a slamfest between the untouted Ceballos and muscular Larry Johnson of the Charlotte Hornets. While Ceballos had coasted unimpressively through the early rounds, Johnson had grabbed the spotlight with a series of stunning jams. But with a trophy on the line Cedric Ceballos had saved the best for last. Calling the maneuver his "Hocus Pocus" dunk, Ceballos strapped on a blindfold at midcourt and soared blindly at the rim. The result is one that hoop fanatics everywhere still

celebrate whenever high-flying moves are the subject of debate.

Ceballos has recently demonstrated that his skills as an all-around player are also considerable. During his third pro season the stocky but often airborne forward slammed balls through the nets for a .576 field goal percentage, which was good enough to lead the entire league. He thus became only the second Phoenix player ever to pace the NBA in shooting accuracy. And other numbers were up for Ceballos as well as he cracked a double-figure scoring average for the first time in his three-year career and also more than doubled his previous rebounding totals. A player who always had plenty of flair in his game, this high flyer has now proven that his game has plenty of substance as well.

LEFT: This number 23 doesn't play with the Chicago Bulls. But Cedric Ceballos puts on an "Air Jordan" hangtime display of his own in Chicago Stadium as Chicago's Pippen (33) and Jordan (23) along with Charles Barkley look on.

OPPOSITE: Perhaps no big man other than Barkley in today's NBA mixes an outside game with his inside moves better than Derrick Coleman of the New Jersey Nets. A capable three-point bomber, here Coleman settles for an inside move that leaves Chicago's Bill Wennington helpless to defend the hoop.

Derrick Coleman

New Jersey Nets

Height: **6'10"**; Position: **Forward**
College: **Syracuse University**
Drafted: **New Jersey, 1990**

"If you want someone who is versatile and can play any position on the court, then I'm the man." – DERRICK COLEMAN

Derrick Coleman kicked off his NBA career by earning Rookie of the Year honors for a 1991 season in which he led the Nets in rebounding and scored a team second-best 1,364 points. If there is any NBA big man who seems destined for superstardom it is the towering power forward now playing for New Jersey. Respected observers see Coleman as one of the can't-miss headliners in the future of the NBA and have praised him at great length. Yet Coleman has also had his detractors during his young NBA career. Many pundits are troubled by the gap between his reported advance credentials and his

LEFT: The first player selected in the 1990 college draft and the 1991 NBA Rookie of the Year selection, Derrick Coleman was also the all-time NBA rebound leader when he left Syracuse University to enter the pro game. Although he sports an advance billing that will be hard to live up to, it is moves like this that have made Coleman into a devastating force anytime he maneuvers near the hoop.

OPPOSITE: Fans expected the 1993 NBA Finals to be a personal showdown between two of the game's highest flyers – Portland's Clyde Drexler and Chicago's Michael Jordan. And they weren't disappointed. In this dramatic Game 2 action Drexler passes over Jordan to an open teammate. Jordan would prove the winner of the series, but Drexler would have his moments of glory as well, including a 32-point explosion in Game 3.

current daily on-court credits.

Many fans admit that Derrick Coleman has had a nearly impossible set of advance press clippings to live up to. He was a certified collegiate legend when he entered the pro game as the league's number one draft pick in 1990. Departing a four-year Syracuse career as the university's all-time leading scorer, he was also the NCAA's all-time leading rebounder (1,537) upon graduation. More impressive still, Coleman is recognized as the first collegiate player ever to record 2,000 points, 1,500 rebounds, and 300 blocked shots over the span of an NCAA career.

But critics and doubters aside, Coleman is one of the hardwood's most destructive forces, especially when he kicks his game into high gear. During one late-season 1992 game Derrick Coleman served notice to opponents with a devastating 38 points in 39 minutes against one of the league's finest young defenders, Ronnie Seikaly of the Miami Heat. He was again dominant during the 1993 post-season when he averaged nearly 27 ppg over five playoff contests.

The cover of the 1994 New Jersey Nets media guide features an image of Derrick Coleman slamming home a shattering dunk, with a caption promising "more good stuff from Jersey!" With Coleman now revving up his high-powered offensive play this clever advertising promise today seems anything but idle.

Clyde Drexler
Portland Trail Blazers

Nickname: **"Clyde the Glide"**
Height: **6'7"**; Position: **Guard**
College: **University of Houston**
Drafted: **Portland, 1983**

"He triple-pumps, changes his mind two or three times while hanging in the air, and still throws it down with two hands." – **DAVID ROSE**, former University of Houston player recalling his favorite Drexler slam

Pro basketball fans were truly excited about the 1992 NBA championship matchup between the Chicago Bulls and Portland Trail Blazers. Not only would the league's two most potent teams lock horns in the best-of-seven series to crown a new NBA champion. But for the first time in several season – since Larry Bird versus Magic Johnson – the game's two most spectacular players would face off as well. Michael Jordan would carry the banner of the favored Bulls in their attempt to repeat as NBA champions. And Portland would be returning for only their second championship matchup, armed with an almost equally spectacular athletic star. Clyde Drexler would finally have the chance to show that he was every bit the center stage act that Michael Jordan was.

Drexler had long awaited the chance to showcase his talents before the widest possible basketball audience. For years he had been a star player in one of the league's smallest markets. Many nights he had been truly spectacular. Quietly he had put together a career as the Blazer's all-time leader in eight of ten major statistical categories, and as a perennial All-Star Game player. But a stellar performance against Jordan would place the final stamp of approval on his game. A team championship would enhance his reputation as one of basketball's brightest stars.

Drexler would not win his championship round against the powerful Chicago Bulls – either from an individual or team standpoint. The Bulls would manhandle the Blazers four games to two and Jordan would lock up the NBA Finals MVP Award. But Drexler would also have several chances to show his stuff on Jordan's stage. He averaged 24.8 ppg throughout the final series and exploded for 32 points in Game Three. In the end Drexler was gracious in his analysis: "I don't compete against Michael and I don't play for recognition. What I can do for Portland is all that matters." In the 1992 NBA Finals, however, Drexler had done all three, despite his modest denials. He had competed head-to-head with Michael and had held his own. He had shown the NBA world what fans in Portland had already long known, that he was indeed one of the league's most skilled and athletic players. And he had carried his Portland Trail Blazers all the way to the doorstep of an NBA world championship.

If there were disappointments for Drexler during the 1992 six-game championship loss to Jordan and the Bulls, these were hardly enough to dim the achievements of one of the game's most brilliant one-on-one players of the past decade. Drexler has always been head and shoulders above just about any rival who dares to challenge his game.

LEFT: Few NBA stars boast more impressive credentials than Clyde Drexler. He has played on the 1992 Olympic Dream Team, been an NBA All-Star eight times, and led his Portland ballclub into the playoffs in each of his 11 seasons. And no one except Jordan has provided more spectacular "showtime" than the man they call simply "The Glide."

OPPOSITE: Drexler showcases a classic "hangtime" move during the 1987 Gatorade Slam Dunk Contest in Seattle. A year later in Houston "The Glide" would advance all the way to the finals of dunking's headline event, only to lose to Kenny Walker after narrowly missing on three final sensational slam-jam efforts.

Patrick Ewing
New York Knicks

Height: **7'0"**; Position: **Center**
College: **Georgetown University**
Drafted: **New York, 1985**

"You can tell just how vital Patrick Ewing is when you watch the reactions of other players when he's out of the game." – MARK JACKSON, former Knicks teammate

There are only a few true "franchise" players in today's NBA. There is certainly David Robinson in San Antonio and Hakeem Olajuwon in Houston. And some might prematurely build such a case for Shaquille O'Neal in Orlando or Jim Jackson in talent-thin Dallas. And, of course, there is Patrick Ewing in the major media market of New York. Beyond that, Jordan and Magic and Bird have taken the notion of one-man teams with them as they have faded into retirement.

New York's Knicks have built their still-unfulfilled championship hopes around a single towering figure who comes perhaps closer than anyone

to being a true "complete package" in the pivot. Patrick Ewing swats away shots from enemy bombers, he sweeps the boards clean at both ends of the floor, he intimidates enemy forwards and guards who try to drive through the lines, he

BELOW: Dream Team action features Patrick Ewing pulling a rebound away from Croatia's Stojko Vrankovic during the 1992 Gold Medal game in Barcelona.

OPPOSITE: Ewing slams one home on a breakaway in Chicago Stadium as Kiki Vandeweghe (55) and Gerald Wilkins (21) trail after the play.

initiates fast breaks with pinpoint outlet passes that remind older fans of Bill Russell, and he is truly unstoppable when he goes one-on-one against rival centers within dunking range of the bucket.

And there is even more to his awesome multifaceted game. In recent years Ewing has fine-tuned a short-range jumper that keeps defenders back on their heels and which he rarely misses under pressure. He finds a way to get the ball into the net or into the hands of an unguarded teammate even though he is ceaselessly harassed by double-teaming and triple-teaming defenses. And just in case this isn't all quite enough, Patrick Ewing is also his team's soft-spoken inspirational leader – on the floor, in the locker room, and even during rare moments when he makes a visit to the bench.

Patrick Ewing has won many accolades and honors during a brilliant college career at Georgetown and sojourn with the Knicks. He won an NCAA championship and led his team to the title game in three of his four years as an undergraduate. He was the prize of the first-ever NBA lottery draft. He has averaged over 20 ppg in every NBA season and is now bearing down on 15,000 career points. He has won two Olympic gold medals and anchored the 1992 Dream Team. All that remains is an NBA championship ring, which he came so close to in 1994. And even that may not elude the rugged grasp of basketball's most tenacious modern-day center for much longer.

Horace Grant
Chicago Bulls

Height: **6'10"**; Position: **Forward**
College: **Clemson University**
Drafted: **Chicago, 1987**

"The Bulls consider Grant on a par with the NBA's best power forwards. And they have the championship rings to prove it." – JACK CLARY, basketball author and historian

To define the career of Horace Grant after seven solid NBA seasons is to paint a picture of basketball's true unsung hero. Many have said it before. He is certainly not Michael. And he never seems to get the respect or earn the accolades which surround Scottie Pippen. But any Chicago player, coach, front office type or beat writer will agree that the Bulls would indeed be alot less successful without him on the court.

It is Horace Grant in the end who has proved the invaluable catalyst to the Bulls' championship-style play. This is true at both ends of the court and has been true for each of the team's three-peat title seasons. Grant was Chicago's only starter to shoot above 50 percent from the floor in 1992-93. He also led the team in regular-season rebounds and post-season rebounds during the difficult third championship chase of 1993. Without Horace Grant

methodically collecting the boards there of course would have been few teeth in a fast-breaking offense that featured Jordan and Pippen. The key to Grant's game is his mobility and speed, and it is precisely that speed that jumpstarts the imposing Chicago defense. Without such exceptional quickness from their power forward those constantly rotating Chicago double-teams would simply not be possible within their defensive weaponry. And to close out his marvelous defensive contribution, Horace Grant is also the consistent team leader in blocking enemy shots.

He is one of the most talented athletes to play the power forward slot in today's NBA. If he has remained largely an invisible man in the Bulls' championship lineup this is due in large part to an absence of regular rim-rattling offensive moves around the basket. But these too would undoutedly be a showcase feature of so talented a forward were he simply to get the ball a bit more often. So far Horace Grant has been more than willing to put his own showcase "moves" on the back burner in exchange for his role as defensive enforcer. And his team player attitude has brought the Bulls' star nothing short of three prized championship rings.

ABOVE: Horace Grant here demonstrates the offensive muscle that has made him one of the game's most feared and respected power forwards.

LEFT: Versatile Horace Grant can put the ball on the floor almost as well as he puts it in the enemy net, as he demonstrates here with an agile dribbling move around Detroit's Bill Laimbeer.

OPPOSITE: Jim Jackson would have been a shoo-in for NBA All-Rookie Team selection and perhaps even garnered Rookie of the Year honors had he not missed much of his first campaign as a contract holdout. Once he pulled on the Dallas uniform, however, defenses had little success in keeping Jackson away from the hoop.

Jim Jackson
Dallas Mavericks

Nickname: **"Jimmy"**
Height: **6'6"**; Position: **Guard**
College: **Ohio State University**
Drafted: **Dallas, 1992**

"Jim Jackson is The Truth. If he gets his shooting down he could be Michael Jordan." – SPUD WEBB, Sacramento Kings

When Jim Jackson took his talented act into the NBA at the end of his junior season at Ohio State, some thought that this was indeed another Michael Jordan in the making. For Jim Jackson had displayed enough of the same incredible all-around flair during his shortened collegiate career to re- mind experts and casual fans alike of the incom- parable Michael Jordan as a college player at North Carolina. The two-time Big Ten Player of the Year and 1992 conference scoring champion was truly already a triple-threat player. His offensive game was almost unstoppable since he had an uncanny

RIGHT: Jackson entered the NBA billed as the next Michael Jordan, and perhaps the talented prospect sometimes tried to do too much with the ball during his short rookie season. But if he sometimes forced the ball to the hoop it was often in rather spectacular fashion.

BELOW: Jim Jackson began his Ohio State career as Big Ten Freshman of the Year and ended it as a consensus All-American during his junior campaign. Mavericks fans hope for similar honors and stardom at the pro level for the player selected fourth overall in the 1992 draft.

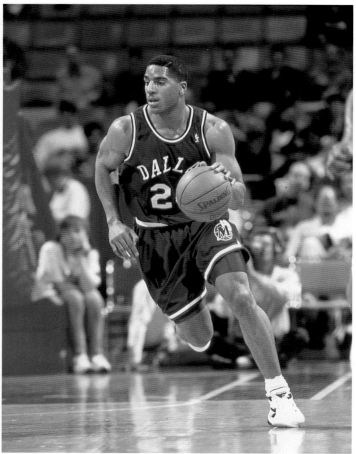

ability to post up, drive to the hoop, or hit consistently from the perimeter. Spud Webb was not alone in his quick comparisons of Jim Jackson and the man they call Michael.

But then a few things seemed to go wrong immediately for the talented Ohio State player on the eve of his entry into the NBA scene. First there was a lengthy and bitter contract dispute that largely ruined his rookie season. And there was the dreadful Dallas team that he joined when he finally did take the floor in late March. Nonetheless, fans and opponents were quick to discover that comparisons with Jordan might not be entirely unwarranted. Jackson made an instant impact with the lackluster Dallas club by averaging 16.3 ppg while starting the season's final 28 games.

The most impressive thing about Jim Jackson is perhaps his creativity with the basketball. He is indeed a true basketball wizard once the ball is in his hands. This creativity is not only limited to solo moves toward the hoop, either, as the talented rookie quickly proved one of the flashiest passers in Mavericks history and paced his club in assists 10 of his first 28 league games. And by scoring at a 20-point clip throughout his first full NBA season Jackson has already become a franchise player after barely 12 months on the NBA scene.

Larry Johnson
Charlotte Hornets

Nickname: **"LJ"**
Height: **6'7"**; Position: **Forward**
College: **Odessa Junior College; UNLV**
Drafted: **Charlotte, 1991**

"How can a big man like that fly through the air, twirl his body all the way around after he'd started going one way and still jam?" – MAGIC JOHNSON, commenting on Johnson's 1992 NBA Slam Dunk Contest performance

Early heroes of the NBA played in relative obscurity when compared with today's high-profile basketball superstars. In the days of Oscar Robertson, Bill Russell and Wilt Chamberlain, televised basketball was reserved for the playoffs alone, only a handful of cities had pro teams, and celebrity product endorsements were reserved for baseball heroes like Mickey Mantle or Willie Mays. Today's hoop stars seem to be more often seen in magazine and television advertising than on actual basketball courts. They are huge media celebrities, and they include premier power forward Larry Johnson of the Charlotte Hornets. Fans in smaller television markets around the country may see Johnson slamming home monster dunks for the Charlotte Hornets only two or three times during a season. But they have certainly seen his gold-tooth punctuated

smiles and delightful performance as video's "slammen-est and jammen-est Grandma ever" perhaps dozens of times.

Yet expert watchers of NBA action – especially those who make their livings as coaches or general managers or scouts – know that Larry Johnson is every bit as much a basketball force as he is a marketing force. Star of UNLV's 1990 national championship team and number one 1991 NBA draft pick, Johnson brought impressive credentials into the

BELOW LEFT: Rookie sensation Larry Johnson displays the form which earned him a runner-up trophy in the 1992 Slam Dunk Contest.

BELOW: LJ finishes with authority the slam which electrified the crowd during the 1992 Slam Dunk competition in Orlando Coliseum.

league barely three seasons ago. And despite a few game-slowing injuries, he has not disappointed anyone once he got there. Larry Bird was one of those most impressed with Johnson's high-octane game. Observed Bird: "He's strong, quick and very aggressive. He is powerful and when he gets after the ball he can jump over anybody."

Johnson's rookie season was indeed impressive by any standard. He averaged 19.2 ppg and also 11 boards per contest, sufficient for landslide Rookie of the Year accolades. His sophomore campaign was reason for still louder praise. Johnson's scoring average soared to 22.1 and established a new Charlotte franchise standard. But like so many of today's high flyers, LJ impresses as much with his leaping and dunking "power style" as with any of the outstanding numbers he posts. Runner-up in the NBA Slam Dunk festival during his rookie season, the muscular slammer is one of today's most ferocious sights, especially when he descends from his patented sky-borne attacks on rims all around the nation's pro basketball circuit.

Shawn Kemp
Seattle SuperSonics

Height: **6'10"**; Position: **Forward**
College: **None**
Drafted: **Seattle, 1989**

"When I was first drafted, I wanted everything because I couldn't see anything. Then I got a feel for what this game is all about – the people who can help you, the people who can hurt you, how to prepare every night for a game. That became my job and my life." – SHAWN KEMP

Teammate Michael Cage provides the best description of Shawn Kemp's virtually unstoppable inside offensive game. "It's like trying to control a hurricane," Cage observed. "You can see Shawn coming a mile away but you still can't stop him." Or as another anonymous observer has put it, Kemp is a fan's dream, an opponent's nightmare, and often also sometimes a coach's puzzle. This agile 6'10", 245-pound behemoth is one of the most awe-inspiring physical specimens found anywhere in pro basketball. But Kemp is also more than a muscle-bound banger. By constantly improving his all-round game he has also become one of the league's most promising future superstars.

When Kemp entered the NBA five seasons ago he was a much-publicized rookie of the rarest sort, one whose previous experience had not been earned in big time college basketball arenas but only in the high school gyms of Gary, Indiana. For Shawn Kemp never played a single minute of college basketball. Only four previous players had ever accomplished the seemingly impossible leap straight from high school to the NBA: Joe Graboski in the 1940s, and Darryl Dawkins, Jim Willoughby and Moses Malone in the 1970s. And once Kemp had leaped over that hurdle, he would also soon prove capable of bounding above almost any defender his NBA opposition could post up against him.

Shawn Kemp was therefore in unique company when he debuted with the SuperSonics in 1989. It didn't take the youngster from Indiana long, however, to demonstrate to hoop watchers just about everywhere that he was more than ready for special challenges found at basketball's highest level. In his rookie year Shawn Kemp started only one of the 81 games in which he appeared. But even as a bench-riding rookie he became an immediate celebrity by showcasing some truly awesome "moves" on the stage of the Gatorade NBA Slam Dunk contest in Miami. As a surprise entry in the event Kemp shocked Miami fans by actually leading the contest throughout both of the first two rounds.

Each of the past three seasons has seen Shawn Kemp's stature grow by similar leaps and bounds in the star-studded world of NBA basketball. Playing in Magic Johnson's off-season charity All-Star Game, he soared through and over defenses for a headline-grabbing 49 points. He has paced his Seattle team in rebounds and blocked shots for three straight winters and has become the club's second leading scorer for the past several seasons as well. During the two most recent NBA campaigns Kemp has ranked with the league's top dozen leapers as an offensive and defensive board cleaner and also as an intimidating shot blocker.

But despite his statistical improvement around the basket, Kemp would only truly arrive in the public imagination during a second Gatorade Slam Dunk Contest, this one held in Charlotte Coliseum during his sophomore pro season. On this single afternoon millions of television fans quickly discovered what hometown Seattle fans had long taken for granted – that Shawn Kemp has already seized his due spot in the ranks of the league's newest and brightest superstars. And it was the action-packed dunking game that had guaranteed Kemp's newfound star status.

LEFT: If Shawn Kemp has a weakness, it is perhaps the fact that he sometimes favors making a sensational play rather than the more obvious and often easier one. Once consistency is added to his game Kemp will rank among the most potent offense stars of the 1990s.

OPPOSITE: Twice in his five seasons in the league Shawn Kemp has been runner-up for the coveted NBA Slam Dunk title. Here he displays his powerful leaping form during 1992 competition in Orlando.

Jerome Kersey

Portland Trail Blazers

Height: **6'7"**; Position: **Forward**
College: **Longwood College**
Drafted: **Portland, 1984**

"Jerome Kersey was hampered by injuries much of last season and we missed the intangibles he's always given us." – **RICK ADELMAN,** Portland Trail Blazers' coach

After a disappointing 1992-93 season, frustrated Trail Blazers' coach Rick Adelman didn't have to search far for some excuses. For one thing he was quick to lament the loss of certain intangibles which a healthy Jerome Kersey might have provided for the Portland team. Injuries had robbed Kersey of much of the season and thus also robbed the Blazers of a showtime player who regularly fired up the home crowd with an array of his super athletic moves to the hoop. Clyde Drexler might be the Trail Blazers' undisputed "prime time" showman. But a healthy Jerome Kersey – in Adelman's view, and in that of most Portland rivals – is one of the most explosive leapers, scorers and rebounders found anywhere throughout the league.

Kersey admittedly lacks the spectacular flare of a Shawn Kemp. He will also never match up to the raw physical power of the NBA's original rim-bender, Darryl Dawkins, when it comes to comparing muscular and mobile forwards who can nightly intimidate defenders with their crashing board play. Yet he is certainly a legitimate slam dunking force inside; and he has consistently proven to be one of Portland's biggest assets for most of the past decade. Jerome Kersey now stands second in franchise history in games played (690) and blocked shots (538), and third in rebounding (4,491), minutes (19,344) and steals (934).

Jerome Kersey entered in the NBA back in 1984 as an unknown small college star who had literally rewritten just about every page of the school record book at Virginia's tiny Longwood College. Although it took the 6'7" leaper almost three seasons to move his game into high gear, the wide-body forward suddenly arrived with a bang during the 1987-88 campaign. Overnight Kersey began looking frighteningly like an unpolished clone of Charles Barkley. Tabbed as Portland's "Most Improved Player"

LEFT: Runner-up Jerome Kersey displays his form and athletic ability in the 1987 Slam Dunk competition.

OPPOSITE: Kersey is an excellent rebounder for a small forward and displays great athletic talent at both ends of the court. He punctuates the fast break for many of his points.

that year, he then averaged only a shade under 20 points, plus a shade over eight rebounds per contest, during the following winter. Though a rash of injuries slowed his game in 1993, Portland teammates nonetheless formally recognized his full value to the club by honoring him with a "Most Inspirational Player" award. And it was little wonder, since Kersey's Blazers posted a 34-16 (.680) 1993 record when the high-flying forward was able to take his regular post in the starting lineup.

Karl Malone

Utah Jazz

Nickname: **"The Mailman"**
Height: **6'9"**; Position: **Forward**
College: **Louisiana Tech**
Drafted: **Utah, 1985**

"Inside the paint is where men are made. If you can't play there, you should be home with your mama." – KARL MALONE

He carries one of basketball's most catchy and appropriate nicknames and one of the game's most relentless work ethics as well. Karl Malone is all business when it comes to doing what he does best – moving the basketball from the backcourt directly into the enemy hoop for another goal. Here is the man who simply has no peer at the power forward position. It might even be said that Malone is the perfect prototype for basketball's least glamorous bulk and brawn position.

Karl Malone is a marvelously conditioned athlete who works hard in the off-season weight room to keep his showcase body finely tuned for the lengthy NBA wars. And over nine seasons the league's heftiest inside defenders have paid the price for that work. "The Mailman" delivers the ball with authority into the waiting nets any way he can, but most often with a bone-jarring power move or ruthless slam that is impossible to defend. In nine NBA seasons Utah's durable big man has averaged better the 26 ppg, one of the highest scoring ratios for any player who has never won a league scoring crown. He has proved amazingly durable – a credit to his dedicated off-season workout program – and has missed only four games over his nine-year span.

What is most often overlooked about Malone's complete inside game is the versatility of his talents. A power move to the hoop by "The Mailman" rarely misses, but when it does a foul shot is almost always the result. For five straight seasons Karl Malone has traveled to the free throw stripe more than any other league player. And the muscular physique of this marvelous athlete is capable of deflecting enemy offense as well. Malone runs the floor with grace, plays hard-nosed defense with tenacity, and simply owns the backboards night after night at both ends of the floor.

OPPOSITE: Karl Malone celebrates a 1989 NBA All-Star Game MVP performance in Houston with this intimidating slam against helpless defender Charles Barkley. A prolific pointmaker, Malone finished second to Jordan in league scoring for four straight seasons in the late '80s and early '90s. Perhaps no other player is more impossible to stop in one-on-one action than Utah's "Mailman" Malone.

RIGHT: One of the most devastating offensive weapons in the NBA, Malone also excels in most other aspects of the game. His rebounding totals have exceeded 900 for the past five straight seasons and he ranked in the league's top 10 in that category during the '93-'94 campaign.

Harold Miner

Miami Heat

Nickname: **"Baby Jordan"**
Height: **6'4"**; Position: **Guard**
College: **Southern California**
Drafted: **Miami, 1992**

"The guy's unstoppable. He dribbles, hesitates, then jumps three stories." – RON SEIKALY, Miami Heat

The player on whom the Miami Heat gambled with their first-round pick (12th overall) of the 1992 college draft soared into national prominence during a single afternoon of the Gatorade Slam Dunk Contest held in his rookie season. Leaping past several favored veterans to claim the dunking crown was a major career builder for the Southern California standout guard. Only Spud Webb and Boston's Dee Brown had ever reigned as freshman slam dunk champions before Harold Miner. Suddenly everyone knew about the rookie who had already been referred to as "Baby Jordan" – a nickname that had come about first because of a striking facial similarity to the Chicago Bulls' star, but now seemed appropriate because of this freshman's budding talent for some truly spectacular aerial maneuvers.

Miner had been a standout college player under Coach George Raveling. He first made a name for himself by joining Lew Alcindor (Kareem Abdul-Jabbar) as the only two Pac-Ten hoopsters ever to score 2,000 points in three different seasons. But several things had caused the stock of Harold Miner to plummet before NBA draft day. Scouts claimed he was a poor passer, his senior-year shooting percentage was unspectacular, and his weakness at the defensive end of the court undercut any legitimate comparisons to Michael Jordan.

Harold Miner's rookie season, however, was enough to put to rest many of these lingering doubts. It was also proof that his notoriety would likely spread beyond the short-lived headlines of a single dunking championship. Miner came on exceptionally strong in the final stages of the 1993 campaign to hit double scoring figures in 12 of the team's final 16 games and to register the third best field goal percentage ever for a Miami Heat rookie.

LEFT: Harold Miner slams the ball through the hoop en route to capturing the league's 1993 showcase dunking title on All-Star Weekend. Miner was only the third rookie ever to win NBA Slam Dunk Championship honors.

OPPOSITE: Charisma is Harold Miner's most obvious attribute, and the NBA world first witnessed that special trait when the personable Miami rookie accepted his 1993 Gatorade Slam Dunk trophy in Salt Lake City.

Alonzo Mourning
Charlotte Hornets

Nickname: **"Zo"**
Height: **6'10"**; Position: **Center**
College: **Georgetown University**
Drafted: **Charlotte, 1992**

"He has creative ability on the court that marks the difference between great big players and ordinary big players." – **JOHN THOMPSON**, Mourning's coach at Georgetown University

LEFT: As a high school player in Chesapeake, Virginia, Alonzo Mourning was rated one of the best schoolboy stars ever. At Georgetown he led the nation in blocked shots as a freshman, and as a senior was the first player ever tabbed as Big East Player of the Year and Defensive Player of the Year in the same season. In the NBA he is already a dominant big man after only two seasons in Charlotte.

OPPOSITE LEFT: Mourning often likes to do it all himself, and in his first NBA game he either shot or committed a turnover the first 12 times he touched the ball.

OPPOSITE RIGHT: Experts agree that "Zo" is more polished than Shaq at the offensive end of the court, possessing a vast array of skilled shooting moves.

A headline Rookie of the Year season is sometimes more a matter of timing than mere talent. Jerry West had the clear misfortune of debuting in the same season as Oscar Robertson. Magic Johnson's rookie campaign unfortunately had to compete head-to-head with Larry Bird's curtain raiser. And talented Alonzo Mourning had the tainted luck to compete for rookie honors with a mega-star named Shaquille O'Neal.

The only apparent flaw in Alonzo Mourning's rookie performance was the simultaneous presence of the huge rival center playing for the Orlando Magic. Another impediment for Mourning was a slow start due to hostile contract negotiations with Charlotte team management. Mourning had come out of high school in Chesapeake, Virginia, rated tops in an outstanding 1988 class of college prospects – ahead of Chris Jackson, Shawn Kemp and Billy Owens. In his freshman season at Georgetown he led the nation in blocked shots; during his senior campaign he became the first player ever named both Big East Player of the Year and Defensive Player of the Year in the same season. Although he missed training camp as a holdout, nonetheless he was an immediate impact player as a pro rookie, averaging 21 ppg and 10.3 rpg.

Potential superstar status seems today a foregone conclusion for Alonzo Mourning, who already has legions of fans. If Shaq topped the rookie voting in 1993, coaches and writers everywhere on the NBA beat seemed to agree that Zo was already a far more polished player than O'Neal, especially at the offensive end of the court. His scoring arsenal includes both a vast array of low-post moves and a soft-shooting touch from the perimeter as well. Although injuries robbed Mourning of his effectiveness during his second NBA season, this 6'10" leaper has already established his game as potent scorer and one of basketball's most intimidating shot blockers. "With Larry Johnson we had our foundation," observes Hornets coach Allan Bristow, "but with Alonzo Mourning we have our anchor in the middle and a player who can dictate the way an entire game is played."

Dikembe Mutombo
Denver Nuggets

Height: **7'2"**; Position: **Center**
College: **Georgetown University**
Drafted: **Denver, 1991**

"Hey mon, have you heard da word? No more flyin' like a Bird. No more Mail delivery. He don't come into Daykey." – lyrics from rap song entitled "Dikembe Block"

Dikembe Mutombo wears a most distinctive and burdensome basketball pedigree. He is one of what now seems a regular pipeline of towering John Thompson-trained centers who stepped directly from the Georgetown University campus into the role of NBA franchise player. First came Patrick Ewing who has singlehandedly (though a bit more slowly than anticipated) resurrected the New York Knicks as a serious NBA post-season force. Then came Mutombo with his mixed-bag reputation. And lastly came Alonzo Mourning, the sure-fire 1993 NBA prize rookie had it not been for Shaquille O'Neal over in Orlando.

Sandwiched between Ewing and Mourning, the personable Mutombo has inevitably suffered endless unfavorable comparisons. He does not, for example, have the shooting range of either Ewing or Mourning. An African native like Olajuwon who also took to the game rather late, Mutombo has yet to fine-tune his abilities to the passing game or to subtleties of evading double-teaming defenses. But there is another side to Mutombo's still-evolving game for which his exceptional strength and natural reflexes leave him ideally suited – defense.

Dikembe Mutombo is one of the most dominant defensive centers of this or any other NBA epoch. Over the course of his second pro campaign he became the first Denver Nuggets' player from either the NBA or ABA eras to surpass the single-season rebounding mark of 1,000. He ranked in the league's top three in both rebounding (13.8 pg) and shot blocking (3.5 pg). And he was the league's second best offensive rebounder as well. And Mutombo is continuing to prove to be a far better offensive player than many experts anticipated. In fact no other rookie ever made the same kind of immediate impact on the Denver club since the legendary David Thompson of storied ABA days.

OPPOSITE: The middle member of a trio of great centers from Georgetown University which also included Patrick Ewing and Alonzo Mourning, Dikembe Mutombo is the greatest shot blocker, defender and rebounder of the three. But he is also an unstoppable offensive threat once he maneuvers the ball near the hoop.

RIGHT: Mutombo is more a rebounder than a scorer by trade and topped 1,000 boards in only his second season in the league. He also averaged 12.3 rpg in his rookie NBA campaign.

Hakeem Olajuwon
Houston Rockets

Nickname: **"Twin Towers" (with former teammate Ralph Sampson)**
Height: **7'0"**; Position: **Center**
College: **University of Houston**
Drafted: **Houston, 1984**

"Dunking is a sure two points. If I try to get a layup, the ball might roll around and come out. With a dunk it stays in." – HAKEEM OLAJUWON

Hakeem Olajuwon launched his unlikely pro basketball career as a mere half of one of the NBA's most celebrated duos of all time. Olajuwon – when teamed with prized 1983 rookie seven-footer Ralph Sampson – made up 50 percent of the famed "Twin Towers" front line that first did battle in 1984 for a newly revived Houston Rockets team. The experimentation with two towering inside post men was destined to early failure since Sampson quickly proved to be one of the most dramatic busts in the half-century of NBA play. But while Sampson's star crashed and burned, Olajuwon's only soared to new and unexpected heights. And a full decade later the talented Nigerian native has evolved into one of the greatest solo acts in league annals. Hakeem has wasted little time over the past 10 seasons establishing himself as one of the game's most dominating big men of any NBA era.

Few could have predicted during Hakeem's rookie season that Olajuwon and not Sampson would one day become perhaps basketball's most versatile pivot man ever. Sampson, after all, had once earned raves with several All-American seasons in the prestigious Atlantic Coast Conference.

OPPOSITE: Two titans clash under the boards as Hakeem Olajuwon battles Dale Davis of the Indiana Pacers in 1992 pre-season exhibition game action at the Cincinnati Gardens Arena.

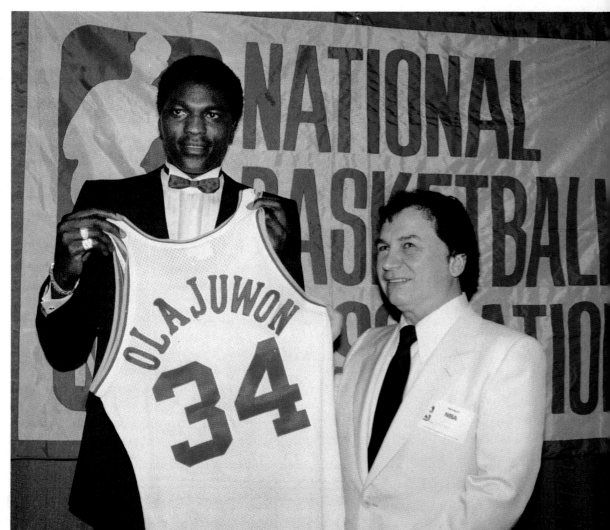

RIGHT: The most important moment in Houston Rockets history came in June 1984 when Olajuwon was introduced as the overall number one pick of the 1984 college draft. Ten years later, as regular season and playoff MVP, Olajuwon would bring the NBA Championship title to the Rockets.

Despite leading Houston's Cougars to three straight NCAA Final Four appearances, Olajuwon on the other hand was a mere basketball novice during his own All-American collegiate years. The former Nigerian soccer goalie had taken up the sport only three years before enrolling at Houston. He was still in the process of learning basketball fundamentals at the same time he was earning his first NBA paychecks. But Olajuwon seems to learn faster than almost anyone who has ever dribbled a basketball.

The NBA career of Hakeem Olajuwon began with a bang, then elevated still further to a virtual explosion of rebounding, slam dunking and shot blocking firepower. As a 1984-85 novice he averaged 20.6 ppg and claimed the runner-up spot behind Michael Jordan in Rookie of the Year balloting. He soon proved the quickest pivot man since Bill Russell, leading his team in steals in seven of his first eight NBA campaigns. In 1989 he established an NBA first with over 200 steals and 200 blocked shots in a single season. In 1990 he became the second player ever to grab 1,000 rebounds and block 300 shots in a season. And he is now only the third player in NBA annals to record 10,000 points, pull

ABOVE LEFT: Olajuwon has averaged better than 11 rebounds per game across his NBA career. He is also perhaps the league's best NBA shot blocker, and scores and passes as well as any center in the game.

ABOVE: Hakeem is more than a mere one-dimensional dunker. He is only the third player ever to record 10,000 points, grab 5,000 rebounds and execute 1,000 steals during NBA play.

down 5,000 rebounds, and cross the 1,000 threshold in steals, assists and blocked shots. Only Kareem Abdul-Jabbar and Julius Erving have reached such a plateau before Hakeem Olajuwon.

Many an NBA rim has been rattled by a jarring Olajuwon dunk, sending defenders back on their heels and inspiring pure crowd frenzy. In 1994 Olajuwon and the Rockets arrived, winning the NBA championship title as the big center took regular and post-season MVP honors. Few others can match his quickness or raw leaping ability, and few have ever played with Olajuwon's nightly intensity at both ends of the floor. And no center since Wilt Chamberlain has had the same soft touch on jump shots taken a dozen or more feet from the basket.

Shaquille O'Neal
Orlando Magic

Nickname: **"Shaq"** (**"Shaq Attaq"**)
Height: **7'1"**; Position: **Center**
College: **Louisiana State University**
Drafted: **Orlando, 1992**

"I've never seen a player with his physical talent. . . . Shaquille is definitely more physical than Bill Russell ever was." – **TOM HEINSOHN**, Boston Celtics TV announcer and former teammate of Bill Russell on the dynasty Boston Celtics teams of the 1960s

He is one of today's most popular celebrity athletes and his "Shaq Attaq" style of slam-dunking play now terrorizes helpless NBA defenders from New York to Los Angeles to San Antonio. In only two brief seasons he has become not only the sport's most glamorous new superstar – inheriting that mantle from the recently retired Magic Johnson and Michael Jordan – but has emerged overnight as the nation's premier marketing fixture as well. The Shaq is every bit as omnipresent in television and magazine commercials, on video (as star of the popular movie *Blue Chips*) and over the radio airwaves (with his own rap music recording) as he is on the hardwood floors across America.

No NBA rookie since Michael Jordan in 1984 has had a bigger impact than Shaquille O'Neal of the

RIGHT: Shaquille O'Neal demonstrates one of his powerful slams against the Sixers during '92-'93 rookie season action. Two backboards have already fallen victim to his super slams, and his inside game is altogether unstoppable once he and the ball converge near the hoop.

Orlando Magic. As Rookie of the Year and the first novice to play in the league's All-Star Game since Jordan, Shaq has been shattering backboards and also shattering records (he already holds all major scoring and rebounding records for his Orlando team) since his very first weekend in the league. Like Air Jordan, he has also emerged as an over-night corporate mega-success, a slam dunking one-man conglomerate whose exploding salary and commercial endorsements (athletic shoes, soft drinks, sportswear, and a movie) earn him more than $70 million a year.

The enormous center out of Louisiana State University (he is 7'1" and more than 20 pounds heavier

OPPOSITE: Shaq was the type of rookie phenom the league had not seen in years. He ran away with Rookie of the Year honors, receiving all but two of 98 votes for the award. He led the expansion Orlando Magic to 20 more wins than a season earlier. And he wrecked defenses with inside moves like this one that sent opponents ducking for cover.

RIGHT: Even rugged shot blockers like Denver's Dikembe Mutombo are set back on their heels once Shaq has the ball inside and unleashes one of his coiling spins toward the hoop. And this young player is still just learning the game, with little in his offensive arsenal besides his monster dunks.

LEFT: This gentle giant quickly replaced Michael Jordan as the sports world's most recognizable and marketable face. Shaq is today a movie star, a rap music star, and a fixture in the world of commercial endorsements.

OPPOSITE: It hasn't all been smooth sailing, however, for basketball's latest and greatest celebrity. Jealous fellow NBA stars double- and triple-teamed Shaq at the 1994 NBA All-Star Game in Minneapolis, shutting down his predictable offense and turning the contest into a nightmare outing for the popular young Orlando Magic center.

LEFT: Shaq runs the floor with unprecedented speed for a player his size and often finishes off a fast break like this one against the Portland Trail Blazers. Such athletic talent has turned O'Neal into a box office smash and thus made the Orlando Magic the NBA's second biggest drawing card on the road, after the Chicago Bulls.

than Chamberlain or Jabbar) combines his imposing size with unbeatable power and explosive quickness. The combination has already brought him to the top of the heap in NBA scoring (averaging nearly 30 points a game throughout his second season), rebounding, blocked shots, and field goal percentage. Here indeed is the most imposing big man to strut his stuff in NBA arenas since the 1960s-era Golden Age of Wilt Chamberlain and Bill Russell. Shaq has reversed the trend of two decades of fast-breaking guards and sharpshooting forwards by singlehandedly bringing the "low post player" back into prominence as professional basketball's most glamorous fixture.

Amazingly Shaq has largely lived up to the unprecedented hype heralding his arrival into the NBA, and his star quality continues to light up professional basketball and heap glory upon the sport – even in the shadows cast by the sudden departure of Michael Jordan. He has also become something of an icon to today's MTV-generation youth. In addition to Shaq's enormous visibility in television commercials, to which he brings his own special brand of charisma and humor, he enjoys a best-selling rap CD called "Shaq Diesel" and performs in music videos seen regularly on MTV. His bubblegum cards and collectibles are the hottest items of today's sports memorabilia marketplace. He has starred in a Hollywood film about college basketball recruiting and been subject of three unauthorized and one authorized best-selling biographies. Though still a youngster, Shaquille O'Neal has indeed wasted no time in doing the things other people merely dream about.

Scottie Pippen
Chicago Bulls

Height: **6'7"**; Position: **Forward**
College: **University of Central Arkansas**
Drafted: **Seattle, 1987**

"I jam . . . therefore I am." – SCOTTIE PIPPEN

No NBA potential superstar has ever been quite so victimized by playing within the lengthy shadow of a teammate – unless perhaps it was Bob Cousy under Bill Russell, or Hal Greer under Wilt Chamberlain, or perhaps Jerry Lucas under Oscar Robertson.

It is not easy to play on the same team with basketball's greatest living legend. Scottie Pippen found that out soon after he joined the Chicago Bulls in 1987 as a small school All-American from tiny Central Arkansas. It was immediately obvious even in that 1987 rookie season that Pippen was des-

RIGHT: On most NBA teams Scottie Pippen would long ago have become a true franchise player. It is certainly one of the very best measures of Pippen's greatness that he became a superstar in his own right on a team that already had the biggest star player in the game's history – Michael Jordan.

OPPOSITE: Shaquille O'Neal descends from another airborne "Shaq Attaq" dunk, this one in Atlanta's Omni Arena. As a rookie Shaq was the only player in the entire NBA to finish in the league's top 10 in scoring, rebounding, field goal percentage, and blocked shots.

tined to rank someday among basketball's brightest stars. With a range of acrobatic moves to the basket and the reputation as an electrifying finisher once he approached the net, he was a player of almost unmatched offensive skills. Yet few appreciated what a rare talent Pippen truly was.

Everyone who came to see the Bulls play at Chicago Stadium or watched them on television seemed to see only one Bull in action – Michael Jordan.

But if Scottie Pippen was a great player and largely an unappreciated player, he was also a remarkably unselfish team contributor. In an era when athletes often focus on personal stats and sulk or complain if they do not get the headlines they think they deserve, Pippen was altogether different. He played hard and anchored Chicago's great teams of the early 1990s in every way he could. He became a fixture in the annual All-Star Game, and competed on the 1992 U.S. Olympic Dream Team.

The 1993-94 NBA season opened with Michael Jordan unexpectedly retiring from the NBA scene. Jordan had walked away from the sport in his prime and now Pippen was left behind to lead the Bulls alone and finally to seize his own share of deferred glory. And when the league's best players gathered for the 1994 All-Star Game in Minnesota Scottie Pippen was thus primed to make a clear and lasting statement.

Arriving on the Target Center floor for pre-game warmups, Pippen could hardly be missed. He was wearing special fire-engine red Nike shoes (Michael Jordan's own brand) which seemed to proclaim that he was now demanding the full spotlight for himself. And as action unfolded in the annual showcase exhibition contest Pippen indeed seemed to be in that spotlight almost constantly. The 1994 All-Star Game was a fitting stage for the Bulls' new number one man to control the action and claim his rightful spot at the head of the league's superstars.

Performing a five-star solo act in the midst of a full stage of "prime time players," Air Jordan's former understudy scored a game-high 29 points as he shot 9 for 15 and also grabbed 11 crucial rebounds. Pippen also fittingly canned a difficult base-line jumper with only minutes remaining in the contest to secure a 127-118 victory for his underdog East All-Star squad. This time around it was Scottie Pippen and not Michael Jordan who was the consensus NBA All-Star Game MVP. The mantle had been duly passed and a new basketball prince had finally been spectacularly crowned.

LEFT: Pippen was a first-round draft pick of the Seattle SuperSonics in 1987, but he was traded immediately to the Bulls who wanted to surround Michael Jordan with the talent needed to win a league championship.

OPPOSITE: Number 33 for the Bulls is an acrobatic player with a full arsenal of lethal moves to the basket. He is also an electrifying finisher once he breaks loose anywhere near the hoop.

Isaiah Rider
Minnesota Timberwolves

Nickname: **Isaiah "Don't Call Me J.R." Rider**
Height: **6'5"**; Position: **Guard-Forward**
College: **Odessa Antelope Valley JC; UNLV**
Drafted: **Minnesota, 1993**

"He's a big-time talent. He comes to play every night on both ends of the floor, and he can jump right out of the gym. He skies over people and gets his shots off." – KEITH GRANT, Dallas Mavericks Director of Scouting

"Trash talking" has become a personalized signature of NBA players, one that is unfortunately imitated as much as jump shots and behind-the-back dribbles by playground youngsters from New York to Chicago to Los Angeles. Many players seek to gain the edge over their rivals through a constant stream of on-court boasts and taunts. It is all seemingly harmless enough and has indeed become a recognized element in the culture of the game.

Such self-promotion is usually private and reaches the ears of only those fans fortunate enough to own a near courtside seat. One brash NBA rookie, however, set a new standard for public self-promotion at the 1993 NBA Draft Day festivities.

Isaiah Rider, fifth overall selection of the lowly Minnesota Timberwolves, raised more than a few eyebrows when he stepped to the microphones shortly after his first-round selection and made an outrageous promise to expansion-weary T-Wolves fans. Rider let it be known that he would reign as NBA Slam Dunk champion during the coming year's competition, scheduled to be played out before these same Minnesota fans in the spacious new Target Center Arena, home floor of the Wolves.

It was a big promise and a tall order to fill for the UNLV star and 1993 Big West Conference Player of the Year. Rider had indeed won a collegiate version of the slam dunkfest his senior year with the Rebels, but that was not at all the same as outleaping and outshining such experienced dunking masters as Seattle's Shawn Kemp, or Chicago's newly crowned prince of flight Scottie Pippen, or Miami's defending champion slammer Harold "Baby Jordan" Miner. And Isaiah Rider had no way to know six months in advance whether he would even be picked to perform in the showcase All-Star Weekend event.

But the Wolves' rookie soon proved to have the true mark of one of the game's great trash talkers – the ability to back up his words with deeds even more outrageous than the boasts. The 1994 Slam Dunk contest lineup did indeed include Isaiah Rider, and the high-flying rookie disappointed neither himself nor the excitement-starved Minnesota faithful. Even experienced NBA stars such as Pippen, Wilkins and Ewing leaped with excitement from their sideline seats when Isaiah "Don't Call Me J.R." Rider pulled off his secret weapon, a thrilling between-the-legs "East Bay Funk Dunk" he had saved for the final round of competition. It was a slam that set new standards for creativity and would surely be remembered as one of the sport's great showboating moments. Suddenly the NBA had both a new king of slam and a new king of trash talk, and they were both named Isaiah Rider.

OPPOSITE: This windmill slam was good enough to make Isaiah Rider only the fourth rookie to garner an NBA slam dunking title. But this rookie slammer was hardly a surprise like Miami's Harold Miner had been a year earlier, since Rider had already won a special collegiate dunking trophy while at UNLV. Scouting reports had already claimed that Rider could get to the rim and "finish" better than any other guard in the entire '93 draft pool.

RIGHT: When the Timberwolves selected Rider with the fifth overall pick of the 1993 college draft, they knew they were getting a player who had proven to be an awesome scorer at UNLV and might be counted on for 20 ppg in the NBA. They hardly expected to land the new league slam dunking champion as well.

Stanley Roberts
Los Angeles Clippers

Nickname: **"Fatty"**
Height: **7'0"**; Position: **Center**
College: **Louisiana State University**
Drafted: **Orlando, 1991**

"Stanley Roberts is built like your average five-story building, only a lot softer." – 1994 BASKET-BALL ALMANAC scouting report

There are some ballplayers that fans just love to hate and Stanley Roberts seems to attract detractors and nay-sayers the way Magic Johnson or Michael Jordan attract "hosannas." The problem in large part is that Roberts has never lived up to the inflated expectations that marked his early career. And it hasn't helped either that the on-court and off-court behavior of the towering Los Angeles Clippers center has fostered a popular impression of a somewhat spoiled athlete who demonstrates surprisingly little pride in his own level of performance.

Roberts made it through only one season as Shaquille O'Neal's teammate on a powerful LSU college team before falling victim to career-ending academic problems. After a season of professional basketball in Spain the seven-footer entered the NBA with the Orlando Magic and earned a small measure of respectability with a 10-point scoring average and NBA all-rookie-team honors. Yet

LEFT: Stanley Roberts has often been maligned, thought of by some as the NBA's most disappointing underachiever. But in the 1992-93 season he jammed 150 dunks, trailing only rookies Shaquille O'Neal and Alonzo Mourning among the league's most active slammers.

OPPOSITE: An oversized body may have slowed Roberts's abilities to move up and down the court, especially on defense. But bulk has not prevented the Clippers' 7-foot center from regularly and effectively going airborne.

Roberts missed 20 rookie games due to injury and was criticized for "soft" play against the league's better and bulkier post players. Unloaded to the Clippers when Shaq arrived in Orlando, Roberts also turned in a sub-par sophomore campaign distinguished only by his league-high totals in personal fouls and disqualifications.

Yet the negative press clippings which seem so far to have overwhelmed Roberts's pro basketball career are not enough to eclipse the considerable potential of one of the game's most imposing wide-bodies. When motivated – or perhaps when riled by taunting crowds or aggressive defenders – the Clippers' "man in the middle" can suddenly turn in some of basketball's hottest crowd-pleasing jam sessions. For one thing he threw down a club-high 150 slam dunks last season which was good enough for third best in the league. Mostly what seems missing from Roberts's game is a small dose of ball-handling skill and better physical conditioning.

David Robinson

San Antonio Spurs

Nickname: **"The Admiral"**
Height: **7'1"**; Position: **Center**
College: **United States Naval Academy**
Drafted: **San Antonio, 1987**

"All the moves have been made thousands of times before, and everything you play has already been played. But you're doing it with your own flair, and that makes it all yours. You see, it's not really for anybody else. It's for me, just for me." – **DAVID ROBINSON**, speaking of both basketball and his other passion, jazz

If David Robinson ranks a few notches behind Hakeem Olajuwon and Patrick Ewing as the greatest contemporary center it is only because of a subtle difference in style. Olajuwon and Ewing are traditional post-men who employ bulk and brawn to intimidate and to totally control the zone that extends five to ten feet from the basket. David Robinson is a more mobile big man, one who will entice his counterpart into a no-man's land near the top of the paint and then bury him with a series of deadly jumpers, hooks and fadeaways. It is a technique that was good enough to allow "The Admiral" to

LEFT: Dream Team center David Robinson shows off his dunking style during Team USA's 1992 "Tour of the Americas" game action versus Canada. Olympic play allowed fans around the world to see The Admiral demonstrate a physique and a smooth-as-silk offensive technique that are the envy of all other NBA big men both past and present.

OPPOSITE: The Admiral hangs on the rim after a slam during 1993 All-Star Game action in Utah. Not only has Robinson played in the NBA All-Star Game in each of his first five seasons, but he has also played on two U.S. Olympic teams, was the first player selected in the 1987 NBA draft, and earned Rookie of the Year honors in 1990.

emerge as the first NBA scoring leader at the dawn of the post-Jordan NBA era.

But this is not to suggest that David Robinson's game is at all soft or non-physical. Here indeed is one of the most intimidating defensive bruisers the league has seen in years. The towering ex-Navy All-American is the Spurs' all-time leader in blocked shots, a category in which he already ranks 23rd in NBA history and 12th among active players. In 1992 he was the only post-position player in the league to rank in the top five in steals. And his trophy case includes an award as 1992 NBA Defensive Player of the Year.

The reason, of course, that Robinson prefers to clear out of the clogged traffic lanes and face the hoop has everything to do with his special brand of talent. The big man's perimeter game is best suited to exploit most fully his truest asset – his lightning-like quickness from the low-post position. Given room to operate, he can unleash cat-like spin moves to the hoop that no 7-foot defender can hope to block. When he doesn't sink such a shot he at least winds up on the foul line in most cases, spending more time in '93-'94 at the charity stripe than anyone except Karl Malone.

David Robinson's versatile state-of-the-art end-to-end play in the 1994 season earned him the heftiest NBA salary in a league populated by multimillionaire athletes. Few would suggest that Robinson was not worth every penny he earned.

Otis Thorpe
Houston Rockets

Height: **6'10"**; Position: **Forward**
College: **Providence College**
Drafted: **Kansas City, 1984**

"He uses his muscular frame to bang in the post. The same goes for his interior defense. Thorpe runs the floor, handles the ball, dunks, and does not take unwise shots." – 1994 BASKETBALL ALMA-NAC scouting report

One-time Houston Rockets coach Don Chaney once celebrated Otis Thorpe as a "blue collar worker who brings his hard hat and lunch bucket to the game." While such a "nuts and bolts" player hardly sounds glamorous or colorful, nonetheless these are the key role players that no contending team can win without. Thorpe, to be sure, is one of the most overlooked and underappreciated big

RIGHT: With the bulk of his scores coming off of fierce drives to the hoop like this one in Chicago, it is not at all surprising that Otis Thorpe is Houston's most accurate field goal shooter ever. A .592 field goal percentage ranked Thorpe second in the NBA during the '91-'92 season.

OPPOSITE LEFT: With a full arsenal of shots ranging from power slam-jams to graceful hooks to a deadly fadeaway jumper, David Robinson averaged 29.8 ppg in '93-'94, becoming the first center to lead the NBA in scoring since Jabbar 20 seasons earlier.

OPPOSITE RIGHT: Robinson's superb athletic skills make him one of the most talented big men ever to play the pro game. While standing among NBA leaders in scoring, rebounds and blocked shots, the 7-footer also recorded more than 125 steals in each of his first five NBA seasons.

LEFT: At Providence College Otis Thorpe set an all-time Big East Conference record for rebounding. With three NBA clubs – Kansas City, Sacramento and Houston – the 6' 10" power forward has established a reputation for running the floor with surprising speed, banging the glass at both ends of the court, and displaying ironman durability which produced the NBA's 12th longest consecutive games streak.

OPPOSITE LEFT: Fans are already holding up cards signalling a perfect "10" as sentimental favorite Spud Webb demonstrates the high-flying style which brought him a Gatorade Slam Dunk title in Dallas.

OPPOSITE RIGHT: After pacing North Carolina State in assists two straight seasons, Webb was drafted by Detroit in 1985 and signed as a free agent by Atlanta the same year. Dunks like this one made him the first rookie NBA Slam Dunk champion in 1986.

time players of the past NBA decade.

Performing in the small media markets of Kansas City, Sacramento and finally Houston, and overshadowed by star-quality teammates like Hakeem Olajuwon and Vernon Maxwell, Otis Thorpe has rather quietly piled up a slew of impressive credentials without almost any notice at all. In 1987-88, for example, Thorpe was the league's third leading dunker (behind Barkley and Jordan) and one of but five players to average 20 points and 10 rebounds throughout the entire season. He rates regularly among the NBA leaders in field goal percentage and stands ninth (.554) on the all-time career list in that vital if often overlooked category. Last but not least, he compiled the 12th longest ironman streak in league history by appearing in 542 consecutive

games between January 1986 and April 1992.

Perhaps the emergence of the 1993-94 Houston Rockets team as NBA champions for the first time in club history owes nearly as much to Thorpe's emergence among the league's pre-eminent power forwards as to Hakeem Olajuwon's rugged improvement as the game's dominant center. But Otis Thorpe has long been a quiet force everywhere he has played. He was an all-rookie-team selection during his debut season in Kansas City. Later he was tabbed the Sacramento Kings' 1987 Player of the Year for his 61 consecutive games in double figures. A year later he closed out his career with the Kings as one of just five NBA players who averaged double figures in both rebounding and scoring that season.

Anthony "Spud" Webb

Sacramento Kings

Nickname: **"Spud"**
Height: **5′7″**; Position: **Guard**
College: **Midland College, North Carolina State University**
Drafted: **Atlanta, 1985**

Fans and sportswriters alike had to scratch their heads in disbelief when 5′7″ Anthony "Spud" Webb took to the floor for basketball's most spectacular annual dunking exhibition during the gala 1986 All-Star Weekend. Defending champion Dominique Wilkins, Webb's Atlanta Hawks teammate, was one of a handful of rivals who all stood nearly a foot or more taller than the pint-sized flyer from Texas. True enough that the diminutive guard was performing before his hometown crowd at the Dallas Reunion Arena and had already squelched most nay-saying by propelling himself over every pos-

sible obstacle on his way to an unlikely NBA career. Webb had only one response to questions from reporters who laughed off his presence among super leapers like Jerome Kersey of Portland and Terrance Stansberry of the Indiana Pacers. "I can win this thing," Spud calmly proclaimed.

Dominique Wilkins seemed to be the one destined for the repeat title of champion dunker the very year of Spud Webb's surprise appearance among the league's dunking elite. Wilkins – known as "The Human Highlight Film" for his thunderous slams and jams – would score 99 points of a possible 100 during the final round and thus seemed safe from any serious challenge to his title as King Dunkmeister. But even Wilkins's inspired leaps were not enough once his tiny teammate launched one the most memorable performances in Gatorade Slam Dunk history. Three straight times Webb

wowed fans and judges with perfect scores of 40. On this night David would once more triumph over Goliath.

"Sputnick" Webb would soon be conquering other seemingly insurmountable obstacles in the years following his unlikely victory in Dallas. He would also prove beyond any doubt that he could play day-in and day-out in the rugged NBA. In the remaining half of the decade he would team with Dominique Wilkins to lead the Atlanta Hawks to four straight league playoff appearances. He would be a double-figure scorer in the early seasons of the '90s with both Atlanta and Sacramento. He is a sound NBA point guard whose game is solidified with incredible quickness. It is safe to say that in a game populated by giants there has never been a more exciting skywalker than the tiny aerialist who owns basketball's most perfect nickname.

OPPOSITE: As NBA Rookie of the Year in 1994, Chris Webber averaged 17.5 ppg and blocked 164 shots, ninth best in the league. But it was monster stuffs more than mere numbers that made Webber's immediate reputation with NBA fans all around the country.

LEFT: While no All-Star point guard, Spud Webb is the kind of ballhandler who seems to make good things happen once he controls the flow of play. Here Webb looks for the open man under the basket in action between Sacramento and Phoenix against defenders Joe Kleine (35) and A. C. Green (45).

Chris Webber

Golden State Warriors

Height: **6′10″**; Position: **Center-Forward**
College: **University of Michigan**
Drafted: **Orlando, 1993**

"I feel like the luckiest man in the world. I just hope Spud Webb checks me a lot and maybe I'll score some points." – CHRIS WEBBER, 1993 NBA Draft Day

The Golden State Warriors have exceptionally high hopes for 1994 NBA Rookie of the Year Chris Webber. They certainly took a large gamble on draft day 1993 in order to acquire the huge center-forward of Michigan "Fab Five" fame. Webber was the first sophomore plucked from the college ranks as a number one draft selection since the Lakers had tabbed Earvin "Magic" Johnson 15 years earlier. But Webber was claimed by the Orlando Magic and not Golden State, and thus the Warriors' brass had

to part with their own first selection – Memphis State star Anfernee Hardaway – in order to acquire their highly touted franchise player.

Based on two years of stardom at the University of Michigan, Webber's advance billing seems to be justified. He had won first team All-American honors and been named a finalist for the prestigious Wooden and Naismith awards as top collegiate player. In his two college seasons he had led the Michigan Wolverines to two straight NCAA title games. And he was the first player in history to make the NCAA All-Tournament team in both his freshman and sophomore seasons.

It is a cruel quirk of fate that Chris Webber – like baseball's "Bonehead" Merkle or football's "Wrong Way" Corrigan – will perhaps always be associated with the one play he *didn't* make. In the final seconds of the 1993 NCAA title game it was Webber who erroneously called a timeout his team didn't have and thus sabotaged Michigan's final-second championship hopes. But if Webber continues to rule the boards and display his deadly field goal accuracy close to the hoop (he ranked in the top half-dozen in this category during his rookie NBA season) there is little doubt that he will indeed be remembered for far greater things.

Dominique Wilkins

Boston Celtics

Nickname: **"The Human Highlight Film"**
Height: **6'8"**; Position: **Forward**
College: **University of Georgia**
Drafted: **New Orleans, 1982**

"Dominique is a showman. People denigrate that, but it's important. In the old ABA, coaches used to call a time-out whenever Erving dunked. Don't let the crowd get fired up. Coaches do the same with 'Nique." – **STAN KASTEN**, Atlanta Hawks President

When Dominique Wilkins crossed the stratospheric 20,000 point total in career scoring, only three NBA superstars had ever gotten there quicker – Wilt Chamberlain, Kareem Abdul-Jabbar, and Oscar Robertson. This act alone is enough to vault Wilkins into a position as one of basketball's all-time offensive greats.

Wilkins's scoring totals are indeed destined to be his lasting legacy. He is only the 11th player in nearly a half-century of NBA history to reach the plateau of 22,000 career points. He is now assured of ending his illustrious career well anchored in the top 10 all-time among scorers, perhaps even in the top five if he remains healthy and motivated. Since

RIGHT: Although a severe Achilles tendon injury slowed Dominique Wilkins's climb up the ladder of all-time NBA scorers in '92 and broke his string of six consecutive All-Star Game appearances, his was only a temporary derailment for one of pro basketball's greatest pointmakers ever. Wilkins surpassed Hall-of-Famer Bob Pettit as the most prolific scorer in Atlanta Hawks' franchise history.

OPPOSITE: Fans first knew Chris Webber as the cornerstone player on Michigan's "Fab Five" team that made two straight appearances in the NCAA championship game. Webber earned his niche in history as the first player ever selected to the NCAA Final Four All-Tournament Team as both a freshman and sophomore. Now he blazes new trails as one of the most exciting young talents in a star-filled NBA.

his third NBA season he has never averaged below 26 points a game in any complete year. And unlike most players his size who focus their game on a zone within 10 feet of the basket, Nique is hardly a single-minded dunker or limited "garbage time" scorer. He has systematically developed a deadly outside game in recent seasons and is therefore as likely to drill a bomb from three-point land as to soar over the hoop for a high-percentage slamdunk score.

Yet despite the dizzying numbers he has amassed (22,096 points, 26.5 ppg, 5,814 rebounds), Wilkins's greatness will always be as much a matter of unique showmanship as of scoring efficiency. Like Michael Jordan or Julius Erving, Wilkins is a once-in-a-decade player whose breathtaking athletic moves are what fans actually pay to see. And it is almost impossible to watch Wilkins in a single game without getting at least your full money's worth.

Appropriately dubbed "The Human Highlight Film" for his spectacular hangtime performances, Wilkins has consistently remained one of basketball's most athletic slamdunking showmen and one of its most sensational mid-air solo acts. First in 1985 and then five years later in 1990 Dominique reigned supreme as NBA Slam Dunk champion on All-Star Weekend. Twice more (1986 and 1988) the former Atlanta Hawks' star earned runner-up honors in the prestigious dunkfest, once to teammate Spud Webb and later to his fiercest rival, Michael Jordan. But NBA fans have never had to wait around for such a staged exhibition to marvel at Wilkins's unparalleled dunking creativity. Veteran NBA expert and one-time Detroit Pistons coach Ron Rothstein once recalled a Wilkins slam – "a quadruple pump, twisting, spinning, up and under the rim, over his head and in Bob Lanier's face jam" – as the most spectacular individual move he had ever seen in his entire life.

LEFT: Wilkins sported a new uniform after a trade to the Los Angeles Clippers late in the '93-'94 season from the Atlanta Hawks, before being traded to the Boston Celtics at the end of the season.

BELOW: Dominique owns one NBA scoring title (1986) and three second-place finishes behind Michael Jordan in the league scoring derby.

OPPOSITE: Wilkins is only the 11th player ever to reach 22,000 career points.

NBA SLAM DUNKERS' STATISTICS

Player	Total Dunks	Games	Dunks/Game	Minutes	Minutes Between Dunks*
Charles Barkley	**917 (1)**	524	1.75 (6)	20,231	22.2 (8)
Otis Thorpe	878 (2)	564	1.56 (8)	20,562	23.4 (9)
Michael Jordan	746 (3)	649	1.15	22,247	29.8
Hakeem Olajuwon	720 (4)	526	1.39 (10)	19,673	27.3
David Robinson	708 (5)	314	2.25 (2)	11,872	16.7 (5)
Patrick Ewing	648 (6)	551	1.18	20,070	31.0
Clyde Drexler	641 (7)	521	1.23	19,225	30.0
Karl Malone	611 (8)	571	1.07	21,758	35.6
Scottie Pippen	599 (9)	479	1.25	16,512	27.5
Dominique Wilkins	591 (10)	511	1.16	24,522	41.5
Shawn Kemp	493	304	1.62 (7)	7,952	16.1 (4)
Horace Grant	445	476	0.94	15,634	35.1
Jerome Kersey	355	534	0.66	16,806	47.3
Shaquille O'Neal	322	81	**3.98 (1)**	3,071	**9.5 (1)**
Derrick Coleman	319	215	1.48 (9)	7,568	23.7 (10)
Dikembe Mutombo	286	153	1.86 (4)	5,745	20.1 (7)
Stanley Roberts	239	132	1.81 (5)	2,934	12.3 (2)
Cedric Ceballos	207	201	1.02	3,062	14.7 (3)
Alonzo Mourning	158	78	2.03 (3)	2,644	16.7 (5)
Larry Johnson	155	164	0.95	6,370	41.1
Harold Miner	44	73	0.60	1,383	31.4
Spud Webb	9	499	0.02	12,538	1393.1
Jim Jackson	7	28	0.25	938	134.0
Chris Webber	1993–1994 Rookie (Did not play during period covered)				
Isaiah Rider	1993–1994 Rookie				

1987–1993 Seasons (Players Ranked by Total Dunks)
Top Ten Ranking for each category in parentheses

Determined by total minutes played divided by number of dunks. For example, a fan watching David Robinson over the past seven seasons could expect to see him dunk approximately once every 17 minutes, whereas Michael Jordan dunked once about every 30 minutes. Shaquille O'Neal, by contrast, dunks once every 9.5 minutes he is on the floor.

GATORADE NBA SLAM DUNK CONTEST WINNERS

YEAR/CHAMPION (TEAM)	RUNNER-UP (TEAM)	LOCATION
1984/Larry Nance (Phoenix)	Julius Erving (Philadelphia)	Denver (McNichols Arena)
1985/Dominique Wilkins (Atlanta)	Michael Jordan (Chicago)	Indianapolis (Market Square Arena)
1986/Spud Webb (Atlanta)*	Dominique Wilkins (Atlanta)	Dallas (Reunion Arena)
1987/Michael Jordan (Chicago)	Jerome Kersey (Portland)	Seattle (Kingdome)
1988/Michael Jordan (Chicago)	Dominique Wilkins (Atlanta)	Chicago (Chicago Stadium)
1989/Kenny Walker (New York)	Clyde Drexler (Portland)	Houston (The Summit)
1990/Dominique Wilkins (Atlanta)	Kenny Smith (Sacramento)	Miami (Miami Arena)
1991/Dee Brown (Boston)*	Shawn Kemp (Seattle)	Charlotte (Charlotte Coliseum)
1992/Cedric Ceballos (Phoenix)	Larry Johnson (Charlotte)	Orlando (Orlando Coliseum)
1993/Harold Miner (Miami)*	John Starks (New York)	Salt Lake City (Delta Center)
1994/Isaiah Rider (Minnesota)*	Shawn Kemp (Seattle)	Minnesota (Target Center)

* NBA Rookie

INDEX

Page numbers in *italics*
indicate illustrations

Photo Credits